Success in Science

Alan McMurdo
Ruth Wylie
Series Editor: Jayne de Courcy

Ages 9–11

BOOK 2

Contents

Collins Educational
An Imprint of HarperCollins*Publishers*

The ★3★ Steps to Success ...

Step 1

Coverage of key topics

★ *Success in Science Book 2* covers a number of important Science topics. These topics are ones that your child needs to understand in order to achieve the highest possible level in the Science National Test at the end of Key Stage 2.

★ Each chapter takes one topic and works through it clearly using lots of diagrams and photographs.

★ At the end of each chapter there is a *Test yourself* section with questions to answer. These questions will show how well your child has understood what has been taught.

Step 2

Practice with National Test Questions

★ The book contains three sections of *National Test Questions*. These are past Test questions on the topics covered in the chapters.

★ Your child can do these Test questions immediately after working on the chapters. You might, however, prefer to wait and ask your child to do them a little later to check that the topics have been thoroughly mastered.

Step 3

Improving your child's performance

★ The book contains *Answers and Guidance* to both the *Test yourself* sections and the *National Test Questions*.

★ The authors, both of whom are KS2 Test markers, provide detailed guidance and show how to go about answering the questions in the best possible way.

★ In this way, you can work with your child to improve his/her knowledge and performance in the KS2 Science National Test.

Help with timing

★ As the Science National Test papers are timed, it is important that your child learns to answer questions within a time limit.

★ Each *Test yourself* section and each *National Test Questions* section gives target times for answering the questions. If you choose to, you can ask your child to time himself/herself when answering the questions. You can then compare his/her time against the target times provided in the *Answers and Guidance*. In this way, you will form a good idea of whether your child is working at the right rate to complete the Science National Test papers successfully.

Progression

★ *Success in Science* is aimed at 9–11 year-olds who are in Years 5 and 6 of primary school. Books 1 and 2 cover topics that children are normally taught in school in Year 5 (ages 9/10). Books 3 and 4 cover topics that children are normally taught in school in Year 6 (ages 10/11).

★ To get the most out of *Success in Science*, it is important that your child works through all four books in sequence. If you are buying this series for your child who is already in Year 6, then it is still advisable to work through from Book 1 to Book 4, to ensure that your child benefits from the progression built into the series.

Note to teachers

★ This book, and the other three titles in the *Success in Science* series, are designed for use at home and in schools in Years 5 and 6. They focus on the key science concepts and skills that will raise children's performance in the Science National Test.

★ You can use the books in class or give them to children for homework to ensure that they are fully prepared for their Science National Test.

1 Materials and their properties

What you need to know

★ What are 'properties' of materials?

★ Why are different objects made from different materials?

★ What are electrical conductors and electrical insulators?

★ What are thermal conductors and thermal insulators?

★ How can thermal insulators be used to keep things hot or cold?

This chapter will help you to answer these key questions.

Properties of materials

In Science, the word **material** is used to describe any substance from which things are made. It is not used just when describing a cloth or fabric. Examples of common materials are glass, metal, paper, plastic, polythene and cork.

These materials are all different from one another. Some are stronger than others, some are very hard, some are waterproof. We describe these characteristics as the **properties** of the material.

Properties of the material				
Material	Is it waterproof?	Is it hard?	Is it transparent?	Is it flexible?
Plastic bag	✓			✓
Wine glass	✓	✓	✓	
Woollen jumper				✓

Different objects are made from different materials

We make objects out of particular materials because of the properties of the materials. The properties of the materials are linked to what the objects are used for.

A knife is made from steel because steel is strong and does not bend easily.

A window is made of glass because glass is transparent and waterproof. You can see out of the window but the rain cannot get in.

Wellington boots are made of rubber because rubber is waterproof and is flexible enough to be made into a boot.

Electrical conductors and electrical insulators

Some materials let electricity pass through them easily. We say they are 'good conductors of electricity' or 'good electrical conductors'. Metals are good electrical conductors. This is why the wire in electrical cables is made from metal.

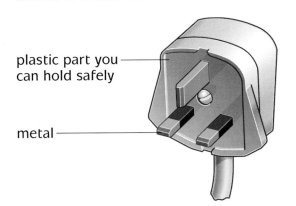

plastic part you can hold safely

metal

Some materials do not let electricity pass through them easily. These materials are not good electrical conductors. We say they are 'electrical insulators'. Plastic is an electrical insulator. It does not conduct electricity well and this is why it is used for the outside of electric plugs. It stops you getting an electric shock when you touch the plug.

Thermal conductors and thermal insulators

Some materials let heat pass through them easily. We say they are 'good conductors of heat' or 'good thermal conductors'. Metals are good thermal conductors. This is why saucepans are made of metal as the metal quickly lets the heat get to the food.

Some materials do not let heat pass through them easily. These materials are not good thermal conductors. We say they are 'thermal insulators'. Plastic is a thermal insulator. It does not conduct heat well and this is why it is used for the handles of saucepans. The plastic does not let heat travel through it very quickly so it does not heat up. If it did, you would burn your hand when picking up the pan from the stove.

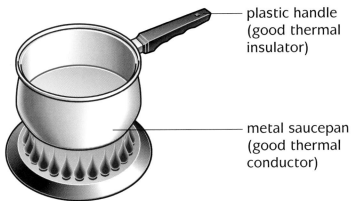

plastic handle (good thermal insulator)

metal saucepan (good thermal conductor)

Using thermal conductors to keep things hot or cold

Some materials are good thermal insulators and this can be a useful property.

Fast food restaurants often serve their food in polystyrene boxes. Polystyrene is a good thermal insulator. The heat is not transferred quickly away from the food and the food stays hot for longer.

Thermal insulators can also be used to keep things cold for longer. Paper can be wrapped around blocks of ice-cream to help them to stay cold for as long as possible. Several layers of paper make a good thermal insulator and stop the heat from the warm air around us being transferred to the block of ice cream which is at a much colder temperature.

Using your knowledge

Which food packaging is best for keeping food hot?

Some children decided to find out which food packaging would keep their beefburgers hottest for longest. They placed thermometers inside the containers and measured the temperature of the burgers every five minutes. They tried three boxes made from different materials. The children plotted the temperature on a line graph.

A line graph showing the temperature of beefburgers wrapped in different packaging

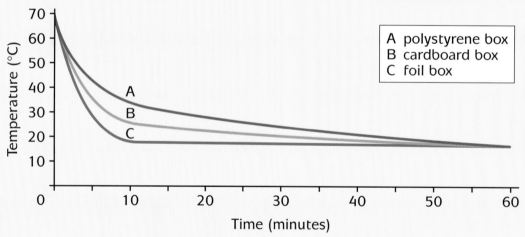

A polystyrene box
B cardboard box
C foil box

- Look at the graph. Which packaging kept the beefburgers hottest for longest?

The temperature drop was the slowest for the polystyrene box (line A). We know this because the line on the graph has the most gradual curve. We learnt in this chapter that polystyrene is a good thermal insulator.

- Which was the worst packaging?

The foil was the worst at keeping the beefburgers hot. Line C on the graph shows a quick fall in temperature as it has the steepest curve. Foil is a poor thermal insulator and the heat moved away from the beefburgers very quickly.

Test yourself

1 Join each material with one of its properties to show how the use of each object is linked to the properties of the material from which it is made. The first has been done for you.

Property	Material	Object
Absorbent	Glass	Window
Transparent	Cotton wool	Cotton wool dressing
Electrical conductor	Plastic	Umbrella
Waterproof	Metal	Wire

2 Fill in the table to show how the properties of materials are linked to how we use an object. Again, one is done for you.

Object	Material it is made from	One important property
Wellington boot	Rubber	Waterproof
Table	Wood	....
Cup	Plastic	....
Scarf	Wool	....
Pan handle	Plastic	....

3 What type of materials are good electrical conductors?

4 What is the difference between an electrical conductor and an electrical insulator?

5 Fill in the gaps in the following sentences.
Materials that let heat travel through quickly are called
.... but
materials that only let heat through very slowly are called
thermal .... Examples of thermal
.... include metals such as iron
and aluminium. Plastic is a good thermal
....

6 Explain how a polystyrene box can keep a burger hot for a long time and can also keep an ice cube solid for a long time.

7 In *Using your knowledge* the children found out which packaging kept food hottest for longest. When the children recorded the temperature of the beefburgers after 60 minutes, they found that they were all at the same temperature of 17°C. Why was this?

Answers and Guidance are given on p.42. *How long did you take?*

2 Magnets

What you need to know

★ Which materials are magnetic?

★ What are the poles of a magnet?

★ What happens when magnets are put close to each other?

★ What types of magnets are there?

This chapter will help you to answer these key questions.

Magnetic and non-magnetic materials

Some materials are **magnetic** and are attracted to a **magnet**. A magnet attracts magnetic materials. A fridge door is made of steel. Steel is magnetic, and when a fridge magnet is placed on the door there is an attraction between the magnet and the steel. The fridge magnet sticks to the fridge door.

Iron, steel, cobalt and nickel are magnetic materials. Most materials, such as paper, glass, plastic, wood and other metals, are not magnetic. Other metals, such as aluminium, copper and brass, are not magnetic. The only magnetic materials you are likely to be asked about in national tests are iron and steel.

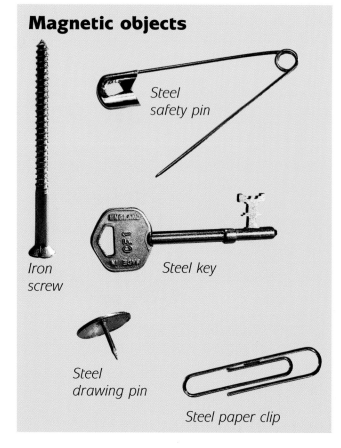

Magnetic objects

Iron screw

Steel safety pin

Steel key

Steel drawing pin

Steel paper clip

Non-magnetic objects

Aluminium drinks can

Leather purse

Plastic biro pen

Gold ring

Paper envelope

The poles of a magnet

A magnet has two ends. We call these the **North** and **South poles** of the magnet. Sometimes magnets are coloured red and blue to show the two ends.

The North pole of one magnet is **attracted** to the opposite end, the South pole, of another magnet. The magnets try to move towards each other. If the magnetic force between the two magnets is strong, the magnets appear to 'stick' together.

When a pole of one magnet comes near the same pole on another magnet, the magnets **repel** each other. The magnetic force tries to make the magnets move away from each other.

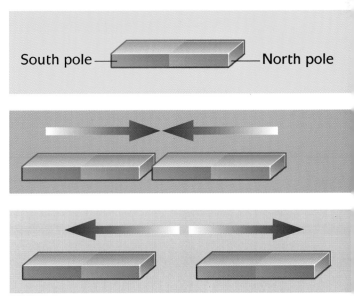

South pole — — North pole

Different types of magnets

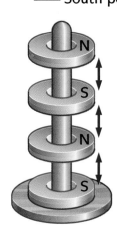

North pole

South pole

Magnets can be many different shapes and sizes.

Some magnets are in the shape of a ring. One surface of the ring is the North pole, and the other surface is the South pole.

If ring magnets have a strong magnetic force they can be made to appear to float. The magnets have to be placed on a wooden rod so that the same poles are next to one another. The magnets repel each other and the force is great enough to stop each magnet falling and resting on the magnet below. The magnetic force repelling the magnet and pushing it upwards is the same as the force downwards due to the weight of the magnet. We will start to look at forces in Chapter 6, and there is more on them in Book 4.

Which magnets are strongest?

Some children decided to find out which of the magnets they had was the strongest.

When a steel ball bearing is near a magnet the attraction between the magnet and the ball is strong enough to make the ball move. As the steel ball is moved away from a magnet, the attraction gets less. Eventually the magnetic force is too weak to make the ball move.

The children put each magnet at 0 cm on the ruler. They investigated the strength of each magnet by moving the steel ball away from each magnet.

They recorded the first position for each magnet where it did not make the ball move.

Shape of magnet	Distance of the ball from the magnet for no movement to happen
Horseshoe magnet	10 cm
Bar magnet	18 cm
Ring magnet	8 cm
Square magnet	9 cm

- Using their table of results, the children were able to decide which was the strongest magnet and which was the weakest. Can you?

The strongest magnet was the one that was able to attract the steel ball from the furthest distance. This was the bar magnet. The weakest magnet was the one that could not make the steel ball move when it was only a short distance away. This was the ring magnet.

1 What do we call the ends of a magnet?

2 The ends of two magnets are pushed towards each other. A repelling force can be felt. Draw the two magnets and label the ends of each magnet.

3 Sarah has made two toy beetles and mounted them on bar magnets. When she moves one close to the other, the one she is not holding moves forward. She has not touched the two magnets together so why does the beetle move forwards?

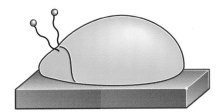

4 Name two metals that are magnetic.

5 What is the difference between a magnet and a magnetic material?

6 In *Using your knowledge*, you read about some children investigating the strengths of different magnets using a steel ball bearing. Another group of children wanted to do the same investigation to find out if their results agreed with the others. They decided to use a different object. They looked around the classroom and found the following things. Which of these could they use?
   a Brass counter
   b Steel paper clip
   c Aluminium foil ball
   d Silver earring

7 a Can you think of a different way to test the strength of a selection of magnets using paper clips?

   b How would you make the test fair?

   c How would you make the results more reliable?

Answers and Guidance are given on p.42. **How long did you take?**

You should be able to complete these questions in 13 minutes

metal knife　　　　**plastic knife**

1　**(a)**　The plastic knife is as sharp as the metal knife.

Why is it easier to cut through the apple with a metal knife?

Because it is harder and won't st snap

1 mark

metal spoon

wooden spoon

(b)　Why is it safer to stir the very hot soup with a wooden spoon?

Because the heat go's up the metal and makes it the spoon hot

1 mark

1996 A1

2 Some children carried out two fair tests on three different fabrics, A, B and C. First they hung a 100 g mass from the bottom of each fabric. Secondly they soaked each fabric in water. The table shows the results of their two tests.

	fabric A	fabric B	fabric C
how far the fabric stretched, in cm	0	6	15
how much water was soaked up, in cm^3	35	52	9

(a) Some children wanted a fabric which does **not** stretch.

Which fabric should they choose? Tick **ONE** box.

A ☑   B ☐   C ☐

1 mark

(b) Which fabric soaked up most water?

....

1 mark

(c) Use the information in the table to give **TWO** reasons why fabric C is better for swimwear than fabric A.

(i) ....

1 mark

(ii) ....

1 mark

1997 A4

3 **(a)** Which **TWO** of these metals will attract the magnet? Tick **TWO** boxes.

iron ☐   brass ☐   copper ☐

aluminium ☐   steel ☐   lead ☐

2 marks

(b) Complete the following sentences using either **repel** or **attract**.

(i) The North pole of a magnet is held near the North pole of another magnet.

The magnets .... each other.
1 mark

(ii) The South pole of one magnet is held near the North pole of another magnet.

The magnets .... each other.
1 mark

1996 A2

14

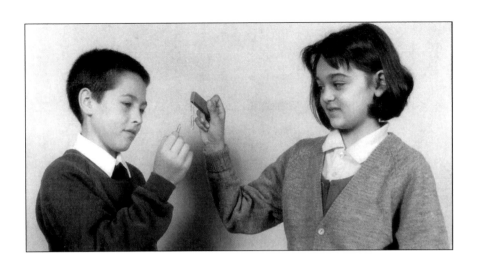

4   (a)   Children tested the strength of three magnets by finding out how many steel paper clips each magnet held. They recorded their results. Look at the results in the table.

magnet	number of paper clips held
horseshoe	3
bar	8
round	5

Which is the strongest magnet?

....

1 mark

(b)   Explain how you decided which is the strongest magnet.

....

1 mark

(c)   Explain why a magnet will not attract plastic paper clips.

....

1 mark

1997 A2

Answers and Guidance are given on p.46.   **How long did you take?**

What you need to know

★ What happens to water at temperatures below 0°C?

★ What is evaporation?

★ What is condensation?

This chapter will help you to answer these key questions. Before you start you might like to look again at Book 1, Chapter 3 to remind yourself about solids, liquids and gases.

Water at temperatures below 0°C

For most of the year, the water that we see around us is **liquid**. Rain forms puddles and ponds have water in them.

During the winter, the temperature outside sometimes drops very low. When the temperature is below 0°C, water starts to **freeze** and turns into a solid called **ice**. Puddles and the surface of the ponds become **solid** as ice is formed.

When the temperature rises above 0°C the ice starts to **melt** and turns back into liquid water.

Exactly the same process happens if water is put in a freezer. As the temperature of the water drops below 0°C the water starts to freeze and turns to ice. We call 0°C the **freezing point of water**.

If ice is put in a place that is warmer than 0°C, it starts to melt and turn back to water. This change is reversible. So, we also call 0°C the **melting point of ice**. Do you remember this from Book 1, Chapter 4?

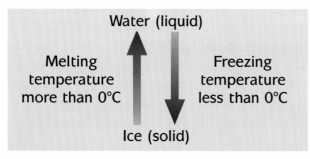

Water (liquid)

Melting temperature more than 0°C

Freezing temperature less than 0°C

Ice (solid)

Evaporation

Have you ever wondered what happens to the water in your wet clothes when you hang them out to dry on the washing line? Where does all the water go?

The liquid water in the clothes slowly turns into **water vapour**, and the water vapour spreads out in the air.

Water vapour is the name we give to water when it is in its **gas** form. We call the process by which liquid water changes into water vapour **evaporation**

If water is heated, evaporation happens more quickly. The heat gives the water particles energy to move faster and move away from the particles next to them, so water vapour can leave the surface of liquid water more quickly. Water can be heated by the Sun, in a pan on a cooker, or simply by being left in a warm place such as above a radiator. Wind also speeds up the rate of evaporation because it helps the water vapour spread through the air more quickly, away from the surface of the liquid water. That is why washing dries quickest on a hot, windy day.

Water will also evaporate from a large surface area faster than from a small one, because more of the water particles are in contact with the air.

Condensation

Water vapour turns back into liquid water when it becomes cold. We call this process **condensation**. The water particles lose their energy and form a liquid once more.

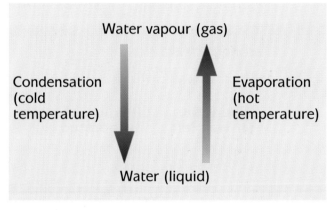

Water vapour (gas)

Condensation (cold temperature)

Evaporation (hot temperature)

Water (liquid)

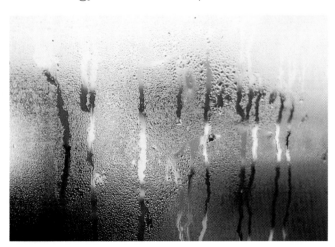

On a cold day, condensation often forms on the inside of windows in a house. The air inside the house is warm and contains water vapour. When the water vapour touches the cold windows it cools quickly and turns back into droplets of water that appear all over the window.

Condensation is the opposite of evaporation.

Everyday examples of evaporation and condensation are shown below.

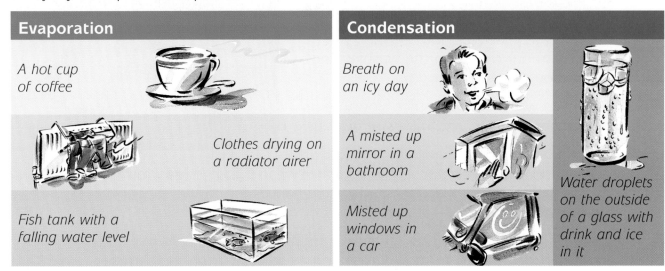

Evaporation	Condensation
A hot cup of coffee	Breath on an icy day
Clothes drying on a radiator airer	A misted up mirror in a bathroom
Fish tank with a falling water level	Misted up windows in a car
	Water droplets on the outside of a glass with drink and ice in it

Using your knowledge

Does the temperature of the air affect the rate of evaporation?

Some children were investigating whether the temperature of the surrounding air affects the rate at which water evaporates. They had three plastic jars of water. The jars were all the same shape and had the same amount of water in them. The jars were left standing in the classroom for two hours.

The children then put the jars of water in different places around the school.

Jar left in classroom above the radiator

Jar left in staff room fridge

Where the jar was left	Amount of water evaporated
	20 cm³
	2 cm³
	10 cm³

After three days, the children went back and measured how much water was left in each jar. They could then work out how much water had evaporated. They recorded their results in a table (above).

● Can you complete the table to show which result matches each position of the jar? Look at the pictures again to remind yourself of the places the jars were placed.

Jar left in outside corridor

Did you work out that most water would have evaporated from the jar left in the warmest place, i.e. above the radiator in the classroom? So 20 cm³ of water had evaporated from the jar placed above the radiator. Less water would have evaporated from the jar in the coldest place. So 2 cm³ of water had evaporated from the jar in the fridge.

1 What is the freezing point of water?

2 What happens when you reduce the temperature of water below freezing point?

3 Which one of these three statements is true?

    A The process that takes place when liquid water turns into water vapour is called 'condensation'.

    B The process that takes place when liquid water turns into water vapour is called 'steaming'.

    C The process that takes place when liquid water turns into water vapour is called 'evaporation'.

4 List three things that can speed up the process of evaporation.

5 Why does water vapour condense?

6 In *Using your knowledge*, some children were doing an investigation to try and find out if there was a pattern between the temperature of the surrounding air and how quickly water evaporates. Describe this pattern.

7 Below are the results from another investigation. They show how quickly dishes of water dried out in various places during a day in winter.

Position of dish	Time to dry out
Fridge	*2 days*
Outside the classroom window	*95 minutes*
Inside near a radiator	*27 minutes*

    a Describe the pattern that links the results.

    b List three things that the children would need to keep the same in order to make the test as fair as possible.

Answers and Guidance are given on p.43. **How long did you take?**

What you need to know

⭐ What happens to puddles?

⭐ How are clouds formed?

⭐ Why does it rain?

⭐ What is the difference between sea water and rain water?

⭐ What is the water cycle?

This chapter will help you to answer these key questions. Look back at Chapter 3 and make sure you know what the terms evaporation and condensation mean.

Disappearing puddles

After it has been raining, you can see lots of puddles. Puddles that are on soft ground quickly disappear because the water soaks into the ground. The water then eventually moves through the soil and rock and drains back into rivers.

Puddles on playgrounds and roads disappear too. But these puddles do not disappear in the same way because water cannot soak into concrete or tarmac. The liquid water in these puddles slowly turns into water vapour, which spreads into the air. We call this process **evaporation**. The more wind or heat from the Sun there is, the quicker the water evaporates. That is why on a hot or windy day puddles dry up very quickly. You can check back to Chapter 3 for more details on evaporation.

Clouds

There is a lot of water vapour in the air around us that has come from evaporating puddles, streams, rivers and seas. As air rises higher and higher it gets colder. We found out in Chapter 3 that when water vapour gets cold it turns back into liquid water. We call this process **condensation**. Clouds are collections of tiny water droplets that have been formed by water vapour in the air condensing. The water droplets are 'suspended' or held up in the air by a force that prevents them from falling. There is more about forces in Chapter 6 of this book.

Rain

As clouds collect more and more water droplets, the tiny droplets join together to form bigger drops. Eventually these get too heavy to stay up in the air and so they fall from the sky as drops of rain.

Sea water and rain water

A lot of the water that soaks into the ground or collects through our system of drains makes its way back to the sea in rivers. All rivers end up running into a sea.

Have you ever wondered why the sea is salty but rain is not?

Water that drains through the ground and then into a river carries dissolved mineral salts that have come from particles of soil and rock. These dissolved salts end up in the sea. Water in the sea will evaporate and rise into the air again as water vapour, but the mineral salts cannot evaporate. The salts remain in the sea and over thousands of years the salt content in the sea has built up and become more and more concentrated. Salty sea water tastes different from the water that falls from the sky as rain.

The water cycle

We can now piece together all the information that we have learnt in the chapter and see how water moves round and round our world. We call this movement of water the **water cycle**.

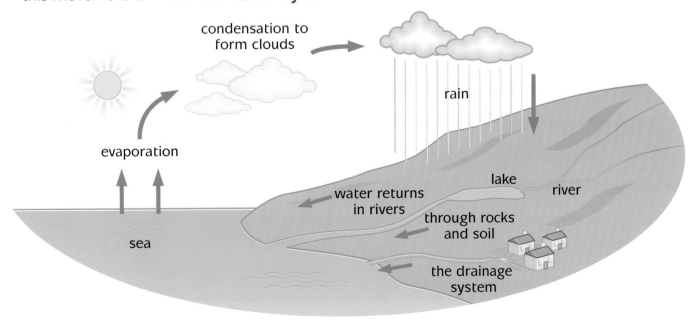

How does a classroom model of the water cycle work?

'clouds' containing ice cubes

plastic green 'grass'

water for the 'sea'

lamp for the 'Sun'

Some children have been learning about the water cycle. Their teacher has been using a model of the water cycle to show how the water changes from a liquid to water vapour and then comes back again as rain. The children decided to try to work out how the model works. Can you?

● The children first considered the desk lamp: why is it needed and what does it do?

They decided that the lamp provided heat from the bulb as well as light. They thought the heat gave the liquid water in the 'sea' energy to allow it to evaporate more quickly. Remember from Chapter 3 that heat gives water particles more energy, so they move faster and move away from the particles next to them.

● The children read the instruction booklet and found that they had to put ice in the plastic cloud. Why is the ice needed?

They knew that water vapour needs to be cold to condense into liquid water. Normally this would happen naturally, high up in the sky, where it is much colder. In a classroom all the air is warm so the children decided that the model had to make the air cold in a different way and so used ice to chill the air.

1 Here are two puddles, one is on some tarmac, and one is on some grass. How will each puddle disappear?

2 **a** What is the process called when water vapour turns back to a liquid?

   b When does this happen?

3 What is a cloud?

4 Why is sea water salty but rain water is not?

5 Name **three** ways that water may get back to the sea after it has fallen as rain.

6 Put these statements in order, so that you end up with the correct description of the water cycle.

   ● **When the water droplets get too heavy they fall from the cloud as rain.**

   ● **Water evaporates from the sea, lakes and other collections of liquid water such as ponds and puddles.**

   ● **The water drains back into the sea through the ground, rivers and drains.**

   ● **The water vapour condenses when it gets cold, high up in the sky, to form clouds of water droplets.**

7 In *Using your knowledge*, some children were finding out about a model of the water cycle. The teacher had asked them to find out how the model worked and to make suggestions to improve it.

   The mountains and the grass in the model were made from a plastic sheet. The children thought they should write to the manufacturers of the model and tell them that they should change some of the plastic into green felt. Plastic sheet is waterproof but green felt is not.

   Why did the children think that a non-waterproof material should be used for part of the ground in the model?

Answers and Guidance are given on p.44. *How long did you take?*

⏱ *You should be able to complete these questions in 15 minutes*

1 **(a)** Gareth pours water into a glass and puts in some ice. After a while droplets appear on the outside of the glass.

> What is the name of the process that causes droplets to form on the outside of the glass?

🖊 ....

1 mark

(b) Where does the liquid that makes these droplets come from?

🖊 ....

1 mark

(c) Gareth leaves the drink on the table for an hour.

> What will happen to the ice in the glass?

🖊 ....

1 mark

(d) Amy puts some ice in a jar of water and stirs.
She measures the temperature of the water with a thermometer every 20 minutes. Her results are shown on the graph.

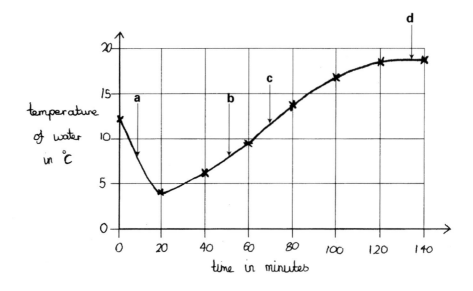

1997 B2

At which point (**a**, **b**, **c** or **d**) will there still be ice in the glass?

Tick **ONE** box.

a ☐　　b ☐　　c ☐　　d ☐

1 mark

(e) Amy is working in the classroom.

What is the temperature of the air in Amy's classroom?

.... °C

1 mark

2 (a) It rained in the night. There was a puddle in the playground. During the morning the puddle became smaller. Children measured the width of the puddle at different times.

Plan of puddle

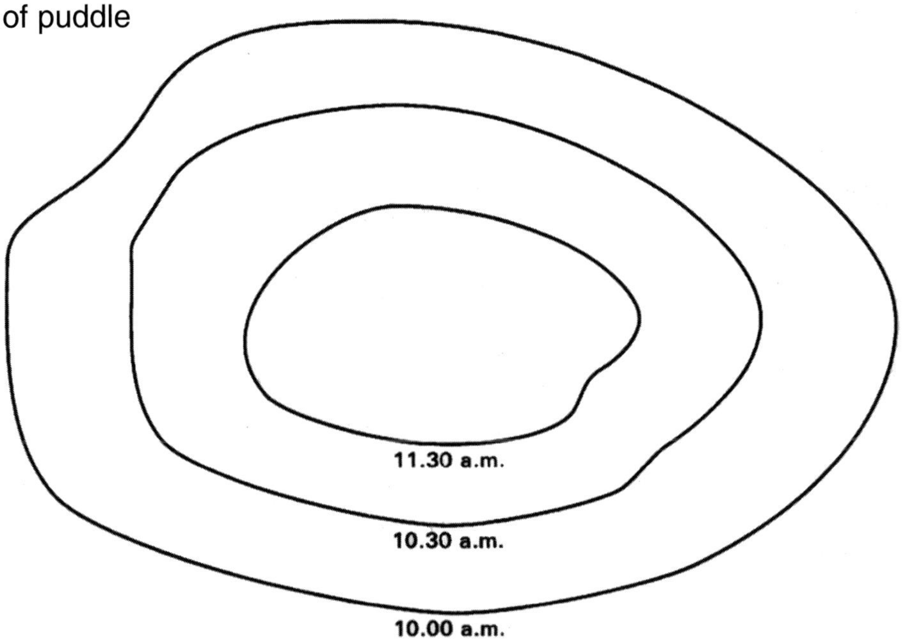

11.30 a.m.

10.30 a.m.

10.00 a.m.

Draw a ring on the plan to show the size of the puddle at 11 o'clock.

1 mark

(b) The puddle got smaller. No water soaked into the playground.

Explain what happened to the water.

....

1996 B5　　*1 mark*

(c) The graph shows how a puddle 150 cm wide changed on a cold day.

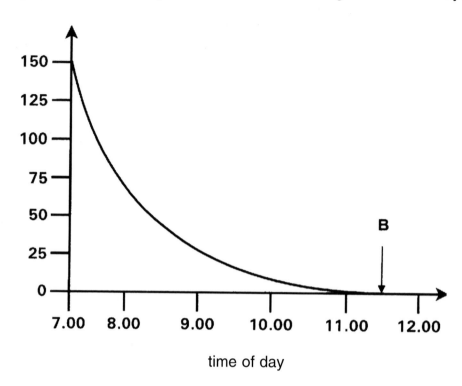

width of
puddle
in cm

time of day

Draw a **different** line to show how a puddle 150 cm wide changed
on a **warmer** day.

2 marks

(d) Explain why the two lines are different.

....

1 mark

(e) What happened at B?

....

1 mark

1996 B5

3   (a) Some children are learning about the water cycle. The different forms of water are solid, liquid and gas.

> Put **ONE** tick in each row of the table below to show whether each one is solid, liquid or gas.

One has been done for you.

	form of water		
	solid	**liquid**	**gas**
rain		✓	
water vapour			
snow			
ice			

3 marks

(b) Sanjay says, 'The water vapour rises from the land and sea into the air. It is part of the water cycle'. The statements below describe a water cycle.

> Write the numbers to show the correct order, 1 to 5.

Write **ONE** number in each box.

The first one has been done for you.

Water flows back to the sea in rivers.	
Clouds cool and water droplets form.	
Water vapour rises from the sea into the air.	1
Water vapour cools and turns back into water which forms clouds in the sky.	
Droplets of water fall back to the ground as rain.	

1 mark

1998 B5

Answers and Guidance are given on p.46. *How long did you take?*

Making sounds

A **sound** is made when an object **vibrates**. When something vibrates it moves to and fro very quickly. Usually you cannot see an object vibrate when it makes a sound because it is moving too quickly.

You can see and feel the vibrations from a tuning fork when it makes a sound. To make the tuning fork work you need to bang the prongs against a table and then stand the fork on the hard surface. If you look closely you can see the prongs vibrating very quickly. If you touch the prongs lightly you can feel the vibrations.

If you want to see the effect of a drum skin vibrating when it is hit, you can scatter sand over the surface of the drum. When the drum is hit, a sound is made because the drum skin starts to vibrate. The vibrations happen all over the drum skin and cause the sand to move and make a pattern.

When you speak, you make the vocal chords in your throat vibrate. You do this as you breathe out.

Hearing sounds

For us to hear a sound, the vibrations have to travel from the object to our ears.

Usually sound vibrations have travelled through air but they can travel through other materials.

If you are sitting at a table place your ear on the table. Stretch out your arm and tap the table very gently with one finger. Even though this tap is a very quiet sound you can hear it clearly as the sound vibrations travel through the table and enter your ear.

The loudness of a sound

Changing the **loudness** of a sound is like turning the volume button on the television up or down. You do not change the type of sound, just whether you can hear it easily or not.

If you pluck an elastic band hard or hit a drum hard, it makes a big vibration that causes a loud sound. If you pluck or hit gently, you get small sound vibrations and a quiet sound. The note is the same.

The harder you hit or pluck something the louder the sound that is made. This is because the vibrations are bigger.

The pitch of a sound

We use the word **pitch** to talk about the 'highness' or 'lowness' of a sound.

Xylophones and chime bars make a sound when they are hit. Recorders need to be blown so that the air vibrates inside the tube to make a noise.

High-pitched sounds are made from the shorter bars on a xylophone and chime bars and from a shorter recorder. **Low-pitched** sounds come from the long bars of a xylophone and chime bars. The long bass recorder makes a low-pitched sound when it is blown. Long objects and instruments vibrate to make low-pitched sounds.

Changing the pitch of sounds

Have you ever twanged a ruler on the edge of the table? You can change the pitch of the sound by moving the ruler.

We have learnt that long objects vibrate to give low-pitched sounds. When the ruler is sticking out a long way it vibrates to give a low-pitched sound. As you move the ruler in, so that the end vibrating becomes shorter, the pitch of the sound gets higher.

If you put your finger on the string of a guitar to shorten the length of wire that is vibrating the pitch of the sound gets higher. The longer the string the lower the pitch of the sound.

You can also change the pitch of a vibrating object if you can stretch it. You can make a drum by stretching a rubber balloon over a jar. By pulling the balloon tighter you can make the sound higher when you hit the drum.

If you make your vocal chords tighter (using your muscles), your voice will be higher.

Which material would be best to make ear protectors?

Some children decided to investigate which materials would be best for making a pair of ear protectors to stop sound reaching their ears. The children planned an investigation testing five different materials as ear protectors: **cotton wool**, **paper towel**, **carpet**, **plastic bag** and **bubble wrap**.

hair band

rings of cardboard

material being tested

They made a pair of ear protectors using a hair band and rings of cardboard. The different materials could be stuck to the cardboard rings. The children chose one person to wear the ear protectors. This person had to walk away from a buzzer until he or she could not hear the noise any longer. The distance between the person and the buzzer was then measured. The children did this test using each different material in the ear protectors.

They drew a bar graph to show their results.

A bar graph to show the distance moved by the child for each material

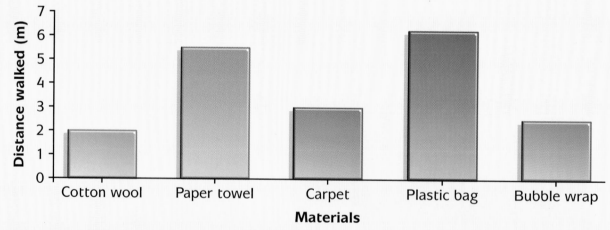

● Which materials made the best ear protectors?

The cotton wool, carpet and bubble wrap were good at muffling the sound of the buzzer. These materials are thick. The sound was absorbed by the materials and so the vibrations could not get through to the children's ears easily.

The plastic bag and paper towel did not make very good ear protectors. They are both very thin materials. The sound vibrations passed through them easily and entered the children's ears.

1 How is a sound made?

2 The teacher blows the whistle. How does the sound of the whistle reach the children's ears?

3 How can you make a louder sound on an instrument?

4 Which of these recorders would you expect to make the lowest sound and why?

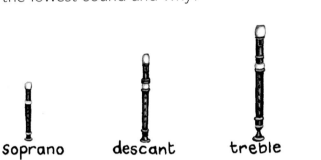

soprano   descant   treble   alto   tenor

5 How can you make a drum make a higher sound?

6 Describe the pattern linking the length of a twanging ruler and the sound it makes.

Length of ruler	Pitch of sound
8 cm	Very high
15 cm	High
23 cm	Low
30 cm	Very low

7 a In *Using your knowledge*, how could the children tell from looking at the bar graph that cotton wool, carpet and bubble wrap were good at muffling the sound from the buzzer?

   b How could they tell from the bar graph that the plastic bag and paper towel were poor at muffling the sound?

   c The children chose one person to do all the listening. Why were they right not to take turns wearing the ear protectors?

Answers and Guidance are given on p.44. *How long did you take?*

6 Introducing forces

What you need to know

⭐ What is a force?

⭐ How do we show forces on a diagram?

⭐ How do we measure forces?

⭐ What happens when an elastic band or spring is stretched?

⭐ What happens when a spring is squashed?

This chapter will help you to answer these key questions.

Finding out about forces

A **force** can be described as **a push** or **a pull**.

Forces can make things **speed up**, **slow down** or **change direction**:

The people pushing speed up a car.

The brakes and parachute slow down the car.

The force from the tennis racket causes the ball to change direction.

Forces can also **change the shape** of objects. Think about the forces you use to scrunch up a piece of paper and make it into a ball. By pushing down on a cola can you can change its shape.

Showing a force on a diagram

It is useful to be able to show forces on diagrams. We can use an arrow to show where the force is and the direction in which it is working. Look at the pictures below. This time the direction of the pushing and pulling forces is shown using arrows. We will find out more about drawing forces on diagrams in Book 4.

The people pushing speed up a car.

The brakes and parachute slow down the car.

The force from the tennis racket causes the ball to change direction.

Stretching an elastic band or spring

The illustration shows different objects hanging from four elastic bands. The elastic bands are all exactly the same size and thickness but they have been stretched different amounts. The heavier the object, the more the elastic band stretches. The elastic band pulls against the weight of the object and stops it falling to the ground. If the object is too heavy, the elastic band will break.

How we measure forces

We can use a **forcemeter** to measure forces. The forcemeter contains a spring. The spring works in the same way as an elastic band. The heavier the object the more the spring stretches. The scale on the side of the forcemeter shows how much pulling force is needed to make the spring stretch this amount.

We measure forces in **newtons**. Just as we measure length in centimetres and use cm for short, we can use N as an abbreviation for newtons. For example, a force of 10 newtons can be written as 10 N.

Forcemeters that measure large forces have much stronger springs. The metal coil is much thicker and it needs much more force to stretch the spring. The scale on a forcemeter measuring large forces would go up in much bigger steps.

Squashing a spring

Have you ever played with a spring and sucker toy? When you push the toy onto its sucker, the spring is squashed or compressed. When you let go, the spring 'jumps' back to its normal size and makes the toy jump.

Springs exert a force that works against whatever is compressing them.

We shall be finding out more about forces in Chapters 3 and 4 of Book 4.

finger forces down on the spring

the spring forces up against the finger

Using your knowledge

How far can a spring launch a toy car?

Some children used a spring to launch a car along the hall floor. They powered the car by compressing the spring (squashing it up) and then holding it against the back of the car and releasing it. The force from the spring moving back to its normal length pushes the car forward. The children compressed the spring by different amounts each time. They recorded the distance the car travelled. The spring was normally 20 cm long.

Length of spring before launch	Distance car travelled
10 cm	60 cm
12 cm	51 cm
14 cm	43 cm
16 cm	
18 cm	27 cm

● The children forgot to record the distance the car travelled when the spring was compressed to 16 cm. Can you estimate how far the car might have travelled?

Your estimate should have been between 43 cm and 27 cm. This is somewhere between the distance the car travelled after the spring was compressed to 14 cm and the distance it travelled after the spring was compressed to 18 cm. A good estimate would be between 32 cm and 38 cm because for each extra 2 cm the spring was squashed the car travelled another 8–9 cm.

1 Are the forces in these pictures 'pushing' or 'pulling' forces?

a

b

c

d

2 What units are forces measured in?

3 Some children have built a model robot. They have attached shopping bags to its arms using two elastic bands that are the same size and thickness.

   a Which bag has more weight and a greater downward force?

   b How do you know this?

4 Here are some pictures of forcemeters. How much force does each object weigh?

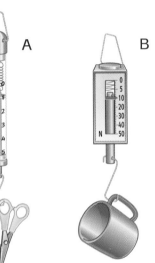

5 Susan forces a spring against a wall. Draw two arrows to show the force Susan is using on the spring and the force exerted by the wall.

6 Look again at the pictures in Question 1, which show some forces. For each picture draw on the force arrow to show the push or pulling force.

7 Look at the results the children got in the investigation in *Using your knowledge*. Can you see a pattern that links the amount the spring is squashed with the distance the car travels?

Answers and Guidance are given on p.45. **How long did you take?**

You should be able to complete these questions in 15 minutes

1   (a)   Ann clamped a ruler to a desk. She pressed down on the ruler and then let it go.

Why was there a sound when Ann let go of the ruler?

....

1 mark

(b)   Jack heard the sound.

What did the sound travel through to reach Jack's ears?

....

1 mark

(c)   Ann shortened the length of the ruler sticking out from the desk. She let go of the ruler from the same position as before.

Describe how the sound was different.

....

1 mark

1997 B5

(d) Ann fixed a pen to the end of the ruler. Jack moved towards the table with a piece of paper touching the pen. Jack moved steadily and Ann plucked the ruler once.

Look at the pattern the pen made.

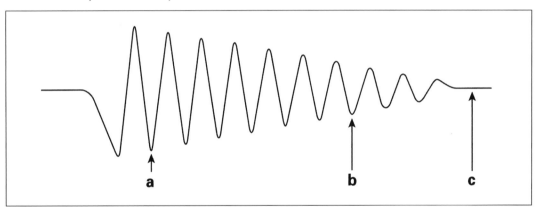

What happened to the loudness of the sound between **a** and **b**?

....

1 mark

(e) What does the pattern tell you about the sound at point **c**?

....

1 mark

(f) Explain your answer to part (e).

....

....

1 mark

1997 B5

37

2 **(a)** Ellen and Michael investigated how four different objects stretched four identical elastic bands.

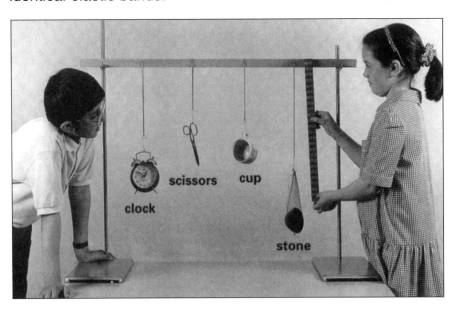

Which object was the heaviest?

....

1 mark

forcemeter

← **spring**

(b) They used a forcemeter to measure the weight of the objects in newtons.

Why does a forcemeter contain a spring?

Tick **ONE** box.

Because the spring is:

shiny ☐   metal ☐

stretchy ☐   strong ☐

1 mark

1998 A5

(c) The children recorded their results.

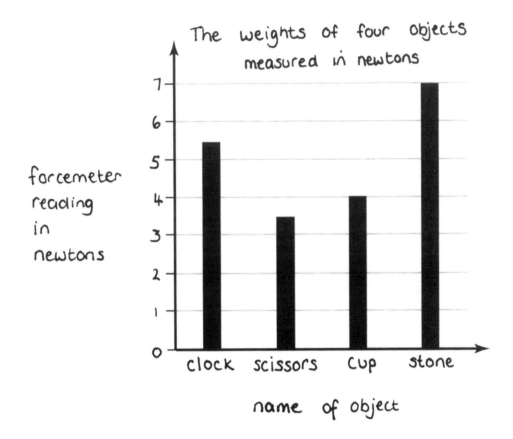

The weights of four objects measured in newtons

forcemeter reading in newtons

name of object

What was the reading on the forcemeter when **the cup** was hung from it?

....

1 mark

(d) Describe how the size of the force affects the length of the spring in the forcemeter.

....

2 marks

1998 A5

3 **(a)** Two girls put different amounts of coloured water in four bottles. They made sounds by blowing across the top of each bottle.

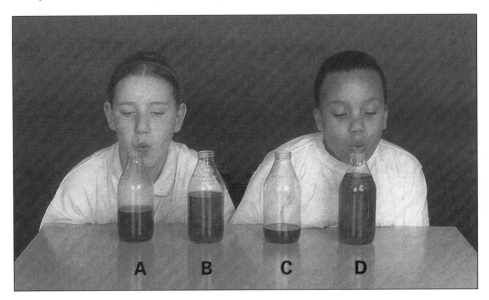

When they blew, which bottle made the highest note?

Bottle .... made the highest note.

1 mark

(b) The girl plucked an elastic band. It made a sound.

Explain why the elastic band made a sound when it was plucked.

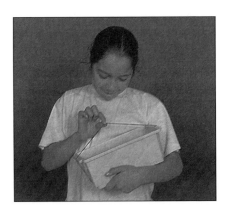

....

....

1 mark

1996 A9

4 Vicky has a magnet in her hand. There are some objects in the box.

Vicky is going to find out which objects are attracted by her magnet.

Complete the table of results by putting **ONE** tick to show the correct result for each object.

One has been done for you.

	Is attracted	Is not attracted
wooden pencil		✓
steel safety pin		
plastic bead		
cardboard box		
copper wire		

2 marks

1998 B2

Answers and Guidance

1 Materials and their properties

1

Property	Material
Absorbent	Glass
Transparent	Cotton wool
Electrical conductor	Plastic
Waterproof	Metal

(Absorbent → Cotton wool; Transparent → Glass; Electrical conductor → Metal; Waterproof → Plastic)

2 This question is asking you to choose the most important property. Here's a list of possible answers:

Object: **Table**
One important property:
Strong or hard (You might have said cheap, easily shaped or attractive. All these are true but not really the most important.)

Object: **Cup**
One important property:
Waterproof or easily moulded (Again these are the key properties even though cheap and recyclable may also be true.)

Object: **Scarf**
One important property:
Thermal insulator (because you want a scarf to keep you warm)

Object: **Pan handle**
One important property:
Thermal insulator (because you do not want the heat to travel from the pan to your hand)

3 **Metals are the best electrical conductors.**

You may have named specific metals like copper, steel, iron, nickel and lead.

4 **An electrical insulator does not let electricity through very easily but an electrical conductor does let electricity travel though it.**

If you said that an insulator does not let electricity through at all then look at your answer again. Electricity can pass through anything if the voltage is strong enough. So if you said that an insulator does not let electricity through it at all, you were not quite accurate.

5 Materials that let heat travel through quickly are called **thermal conductors** but materials that only let heat through very slowly are called thermal **insulators**. Examples of thermal **conductors** include metals such as iron and aluminium. Plastic is a good thermal **insulator**.

6 **Polystyrene is a good thermal insulator. It slows down the movement of heat from the burger into the room and so the burger stays hot for a long time. The polystyrene also slows down the movement of heat from the room into the ice cube, helping to keep the ice cube solid for longer.**

The key to this question is that a thermal insulator slows down the movement of heat.

7 **The beefburgers all cooled down until they reached the temperature of the surrounding air in the classroom. This temperature is called room temperature and was 17°C.**

Cold objects heat up to room temperature when heat travels from the room into the object. Warm objects cool down to this temperature when heat travels out of the object into the room.

Target time for all questions – 15 minutes

Your time for all questions

2 Magnets

1 The ends of a magnet are called the **poles**.

2 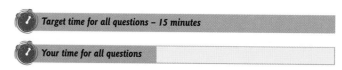 or

Remember similar poles of magnets repel each other.

3 **When you put similar poles of a magnet together they repel each other, or force each other away.**

Sarah used this principle to move one 'beetle' away from the one she was holding.

4 **Nickel**, **cobalt**, **steel** and **iron** are the four metals that are magnetic.

5 **A magnet is an object that has magnetic poles and attracts magnetic materials. A magnetic material is something that can be attracted to a magnet.**

6 b **Steel paper clip.**

Did you remember that only steel, iron, cobalt and nickel are magnetic? Apart from the paper clip, none of these other objects would be attracted to the magnet even if they were very close because they are all non-magnetic materials. So, only the paper clip could have been used for the investigation.

Answers and Guidance

7 a **You could test the strength of a selection of magnets by seeing how many paper clips could be dangled in a chain held by the pole of each magnet.**

The stronger the force of the magnet the more paper clips can be held.

b **To make the test fair, you would need to keep several things the same, such as the size of the paper clips, the way the magnet is held and the nearness to open windows.**

c **To make the results more reliable, you would need to check them.**

You could repeat the investigation three or four times to check you do not get 'odd' results. You might want to take an average of your results.

See Book 4, Chapter 6 for more about 'being scientific'.

 Target time for all questions – 15 minutes

Your time for all questions

3 Water – in all its forms

1 **The freezing point of water is 0°C.**

2 **When you reduce the temperature of water below freezing point the liquid water turns into a solid called ice.**

3 **Statement C is correct.**

A and B are incorrect. The process that takes place when liquid water turns into water vapour is evaporation. Condensation is when water vapour turns back into liquid water.

4 1 **Increasing the temperature makes evaporation take place more quickly.**

Remember that the heat gives the particles energy to move faster and move away from the particles next to them more quickly.

2 **Wind also speeds up evaporation.**

Wind helps to move the particles away from the surface of the water.

3 **The surface area affects the rate of evaporation. The larger the surface area the quicker the rate of evaporation.**

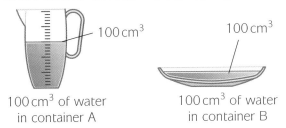

100 cm³ of water in container A   100 cm³ of water in container B

The water will evaporate more quickly from container B because there is more water in contact with the air.

5 **Water vapour condenses when the particles lose their energy and slow down.**

This happens when they hit a cold surface.

6 **The higher the temperature of the surrounding air, the faster evaporation takes place.**

This is a general pattern because it describes lots and lots of different temperatures. Remember, increasing the temperature increases the speed of evaporation.

7 a **As the temperature gets higher the time for drying out gets less** or **As the temperature gets less the drying time gets more.**

When you are asked for a pattern it is important to use the information you are given and not use a new set of words. For example, you might have been tempted to say 'that as the temperature increased the drying out speeded up'. You might get away with this in a test, but do not risk it. Stick to the words in the results. Also make sure you talk about a pattern. If you wrote 'the hottest is the quickest' you would probably miss out on a mark because you are only talking about one result (near the radiator) and not all the results. You must describe a pattern that links all the results. Finally, do not be tempted to write too much. You are asked for a description, not an explanation. If you said things like 'the hotter it, is the quicker the particles move', you were right but you were not answering the question.

b **You could have written any three of the following:**

- **the same amount of water each time**
- **the same starting temperature of the water**
- **the same size of container**
- **the same surface area of water**
- **make sure that no water could be spilt or added to the dishes by accident.**

Answers and Guidance

In this chapter we have found that several things affect the speed of evaporation. The children wanted to investigate how the position of the jars, or the temperature that each was at, affected evaporation. This means they would have to keep all the other factors the same. There is more about being scientific in Book 4, Chapter 6.

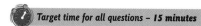
Target time for all questions – 15 minutes

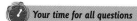
Your time for all questions

4 The water cycle

1 The water in the puddle on tarmac disappears by evaporation. The water in the puddle on grass could soak into the ground as well as evaporate.

Tarmac is waterproof so water will not soak in. The water can leave the puddle by evaporation.

2 a **Condensation is the process when water turns back from a vapour to a liquid.**

b **Condensation happens when water vapour cools down.**

The cooling can occur when the vapour rises up through the air or when it hits a cold surface.

3 A cloud is a collection of very small drops of water suspended in the air.

If the water is very cold, it will turn to ice, so often clouds, especially ones that are high in the sky, are made of tiny pieces of ice.

4 Sea water is salty because when evaporation takes place from the sea only water evaporates, the mineral salts do not evaporate.

The dissolved mineral salts in the sea become more and more concentrated as time goes on. Rain water may become polluted after it has formed, when things dissolve in it, or get carried along by it, but it will not be salty because when sea water evaporates the salt always gets left behind. There is more about this in Book 3.

5 Rain water may get back to the sea in these three ways:

1 **It may run off the surface of the ground and return to rivers through pipes and drains.**

2 **It may run off the surface of the ground straight into a river. All rivers eventually end at the sea.**

3 **The rain may soak into the ground and drain back to the sea by moving underground through soil and rock.**

6 You should have the points in this order. It does not really matter where you start.

1 **Water evaporates from the sea, lakes and other collections of liquid water such as ponds and puddles.**

2 **The water vapour condenses when it gets cold, high up in the sky, to form clouds of water droplets.**

3 **When the water droplets get too heavy they fall from the cloud as rain.**

4 **The water drains back into the sea through the ground, rivers and drains.**

7 The children thought that the model should show that some of the water soaked into the ground and returned underground into the rivers and sea. Some of the ground in the model should therefore be made of a non-waterproof material, such as felt.

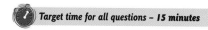
Target time for all questions – 15 minutes

Your time for all questions

5 Sound

1 A sound is made when an object vibrates.

2 The children hear the sound when the vibrations travel through the air and into their ears.

3 You can make a louder sound on an instrument by hitting, plucking or blowing harder, depending on the instrument.

This means you are putting more energy into making the sound, and so you are making bigger vibrations. Try to avoid saying 'by making it vibrate more' because that could mean that it vibrates faster, which would not make it louder.

4 The tenor recorder will give the lowest sound, because it is the longest recorder.

Remember you can make a sound lower in pitch by making an instrument longer. If it is a drum skin or an elastic band, you will have to loosen it to make a lower-pitched sound.

Answers and Guidance

5 **A drum will make a higher sound if its skin is tightened.**

6 **The shorter the ruler the higher the sound** or **The longer the ruler the lower the sound.**

Remember that a pattern has to link all the results. If you said the shortest length gives the highest sound you would miss out on marks because you have only described one result in the pattern. Even if you said 'the shortest length gives the highest sound and the longest length gives the lowest sound' you have still only mentioned two of the results in the pattern and so you would miss out on some marks. A useful thing to remember in pattern questions is the 'er' rule: 'the shorter the length, the higher the sound'. With the 'er' in, you have compared all the results and you would get full marks on the question. There is more about questions like this in Book 4, Chapter 6.

7 a **They could tell this because cotton wool, carpet and bubble wrap have short bars on the graph.**

The short bars show that the children only had to walk a short distance from the buzzer (between 2 and 3 m) before they stopped hearing it.

b **They could tell this because the plastic bag and paper towel have the longest bars on the graph.**

The longer bars show that the children had to walk back quite a long way from the buzzer (between 5 and 7 m) before they stopped hearing it. This was because these materials were poor at muffling the sound.

c **To make sure it was a fair test, the same person needed to test all five materials.**

Different people might hear less well than others.

> ⏱ *Target time for all questions – 15 minutes*

> ⏱ *Your time for all questions*

6 Introducing forces

1 a **pushing**

b **pulling**

c **pulling**

d **pushing**

2 **Forces are measured in newtons.**

Remember that the abbreviation for newton is N.

3 a **Bag A has more weight and a greater downwards force.**

b **We know this because the elastic band has stretched more.**

We found out on page 33 that the greater the downwards force (the more weight) the more it makes an elastic band stretch.

4 **The forcemeter in A is showing a reading of 1 newtons**

The forcemeter in B is showing a reading of 10 newtons

5

push back from wall

push from Susan's hands

6

push

pull

pull

push with the foot

7 **The more the spring is squashed the greater the distance the car travels.**

If you said that 'when the spring is compressed most the car travels the furthest', you would not get all the marks in a test question. This is because your answer only described one result and not a pattern that linked all the results.

> ⏱ *Target time for all questions – 12 minutes*

> ⏱ *Your time for all questions*

Answers and Guidance

National Test Questions 1

1 a You would have scored a mark if you gave a relevant comment about metal or plastic or if you compared plastic and metal. For example, if you wrote '**metal is strong**', '**plastic breaks**', '**metal is less bendy than plastic**' or '**metal is strong and plastic is breakable**' you would get the mark.

If you are not specific about the cutting job of a knife, for example 'it's bigger than the plastic knife', you will not get the mark. If you write 'it is breakable' the markers would assume that the 'it' in an answer is the metal knife; you must be clear about which knife is which. You must also be clear about the difference between the two knives because you have been asked to compare the two knives, for example 'because it is sharp' will not get you are mark because they are both sharp.

b This question is about safety and heat, so if you wrote about a relevant property of wood or metal or compared the two you would get the mark. Examples of correct answers include: '**wood does conduct heat very well**', '**metal is a good conductor of heat**', '**metal gets hot**', '**metal gets hotter than wood**' and '**metal conducts heat but wood is an insulator**'

In questions like this, you must not give the impression that wood lets through no heat at all. Avoid answers like 'metal lets through heat but wood does not' or 'metal is a conductor but wood isn't'. An insulator is the opposite of a conductor but even an insulator conducts a little heat. You would not get the mark if you wrote about other properties, such as floating and sinking.

CROSS-CHECK CHAPTER 1

2 a **Box A**

b **Fabric B**

c (i) **Fabric C stretches more than fabric A.**
(ii) **Fabric C soaks up less water than A.**

You would have got the first mark if you had said C is more flexible than A but try to stick word for word to the information in the table. This question asked you to think about the job of swimwear and how useful fabrics C and A are for this job. There is another clue in the question because it asks why fabric C is better than fabric A. So the trick is to look at the information for fabric C. How is it different to A and how will this be better? A common mistake in questions like this is to say, for example, 'fabric A soaks up water'. What we really mean is fabric A soaks up more water than C,

which would be a disadvantage. You must make a comparison to get the marks. You would not have scored any marks if you had mentioned information that was not in the table because the question asks you to use the information in the table.

CROSS-CHECK CHAPTER 1

3 a **Iron** and **steel**.

A common mistake is to put crosses in the boxes that are wrong, or worse to just put crosses in the four wrong boxes. If you are asked for ticks in two boxes, make sure that is what you put.

b (i) **repel**; (ii) **attract**

You have to use the words attract and repel, so do not use other words even if they do mean the same thing.

CROSS-CHECK CHAPTER 2

4 a The **bar magnet** was the strongest.

b We know it is the strongest because it held the most paper clips. You would get a mark if you said this. For example, '**it holds the most paper clips**' or '**8 is the biggest number**' are good answers but 'it holds 8 paper clips' is not.

c If you said '**because plastic is not magnetic**', '**they are not made from magnetic material**' or '**they don't contain steel**' you would get the mark.

This is a question about magnetic materials. Remember that a magnet will only pick up magnetic materials (i.e. steel, iron, nickel or cobalt) but will not pick up non-magnetic materials such as plastic and aluminium. But if you made the common mistake and forgot that only a few metals are magnetic, and wrote for example ' because they don't contain metal' or 'because they aren't metal', you would lose the mark.

CROSS-CHECK CHAPTER 2

National Test Questions 2

1 a **The water on the outside of the glass has been caused by condensation.**
Condensation is when water vapour cools to form liquid water. Here the ice has cooled the glass, which then cools the water vapour in the air.

b **The air.**
You must make it clear that you know that the vapour has come from the air. It has not come from the water inside the glass.

Answers and Guidance

c **The ice will melt if the glass is left on the table.**
You could have written 'it will go smaller and turn to liquid' but why make life complicated when 'melts' will do?

d **Point a.**
Look again at the graph. Amy puts the ice in the water at 0 minutes and the temperature of the water falls. It is coldest at 20 minutes, after which time the temperature starts to rise. Ice will only be present as the water is cooling, that is at point a. Once all the ice has melted the water will start warming up.

e If your answer is **between 17.5 and 19.5** you would get a mark.

Remember what we said about room temperature in Chapter 1. Cold things will heat up to room temperature, so where the graph becomes level is room temperature. The temperature would only go higher than this if the jar was heated. So put a ruler on the level line by point d, and read across to find the temperature on the vertical axis. You should find it is between 17.5 and 19.5°C

CROSS-CHECK   CHAPTER 3

2 a You get a mark if you drew a ring **between the 10.30 and 11.30 rings**. This is because 11.00 is between these two times. You cannot be any more accurate than that!

b **The water evaporated**.
If the water did not soak into the ground it must have evaporated (turned into vapour). You are asked about the water and not the puddle, so you cannot say it dried up or disappeared and expect to get the mark.

c This question had two marks. The first mark is for **starting the line at 150 cm** (you were told that the puddle was 150 cm wide). The second mark is given if you draw **a line that shows the water evaporating more quickly**, in other words it goes down more steeply and reaches 0 before 11.00. We know this should happen because we are told that the day is warmer.

d **The lines are different because the water evaporates faster on a warmer day.**

e At B you could say that the '**puddle had gone**' or that '**there was no liquid water left**'.

There is a difference between saying that the puddle has gone, which is right, and the water has gone, which is wrong. The puddle is a thing and so it can disappear, whereas the water is a substance which is still exists even when it has turned to a vapour.

CROSS-CHECK   CHAPTER 3

3 a

	form of water		
	solid	**liquid**	**gas**
rain		✓	
water vapour			✓
snow	✓		
ice	✓		

You would score one mark for each correct tick but if you put more than one tick in a row then you would lose the mark.

b The sequence is **5 3 1 2 4**. If you got it wrong, check back through Chapter 4.

CROSS-CHECK   CHAPTER 4

National Test Questions 3

1 a **The ruler vibrated to make the sound.**

b **The sound must have travelled through the air to reach Jack's ears.**

c **The sound would be higher.**

Remember, long instruments make low-pitched sounds and short instruments make high-pitched sounds. You are asked about the sound in this question so use the word sound in your answer. You could get away with pitch, note or tone getting higher but why make life complicated? You would not get away with talking about the tune getting higher (a tune is a sequence of notes) or the vibrations getting higher or quicker.

In the next three parts to this question you are asked to have a look at the pattern the vibrating ruler makes after it was plucked once. It is important in questions like this to read all the information.

d **The loudness got less between a and b**.
We know this because the size of the vibrations got less. You are asked about loudness, so talk about loudness. If you said, for example 'it got lower', you would not get the mark because you could have been talking about the pitch of the sound.

e **The sound had stopped or it was silent at c**.
You would not get a mark for saying 'it was quiet' because quiet means there was some sound, and you would not get the mark if you did not mention sound, for example 'the ruler stopped'.

f ***The ruler stopped vibrating or moving***, or you could say that ***the line was straight at c***.
In this question you are asked for your explanation of the silence.

CROSS-CHECK   CHAPTER 5

2 a ***The stone was the heaviest***.
This is because it pulled the elastic band down the most.

b ***Because the spring is stretchy***.

c ***4 newtons***.
Find the bar that represents the cup, go up to the top of the bar and then look across to the scale that shows the forcemeter reading. Remember to use the correct units, the wrong ones might lose you the mark.

d You should give yourself both marks if you wrote: '***the bigger the force the longer the spring***' or '***the smaller the force the shorter the spring***'.

You are asked to describe the pattern in the size of the force and the length of the spring. Notice the 'er's in these answers. By using them, we have been able to compare all the results. If you just compare one or two results, for example 'the biggest force is longest' or 'the spring is shortest with the smallest force', you will only score one mark.

Also note that both the correct answers use the two variables that we have been asked about, i.e. size of force and length of spring. Try to get into the habit of sticking to the question. If you rephrase the question, you may be in danger of losing marks, although you could get away with 'stretch' for length and 'weight' for force. So, for example, 'The heavier the weight the more the spring stretches' would have scored two marks. Why take risks though, when following the question is easier?

CROSS-CHECK   CHAPTER 6

3 a **Bottle D made the highest note**.
The child is blowing the bottle and the air inside the bottle is vibrating to make the sound. Remember, long things vibrate to make low sounds and short things vibrate to make high-pitched sounds. Bottle D was the fullest so it had the least air. This means that it made a high note. If the bottles had been hit instead of being blown, the water would vibrate and you would get the opposite results.

b **The elastic band made a sound because it vibrated**.
You would get the mark if you said that it 'moved up and down' or 'it made the air vibrate'. But if you did not talk about vibration or if you simply said the sound vibrates, you would not get the mark.

CROSS-CHECK   CHAPTER 5

4

	Is attracted	Is not attracted
wooden pencil		✓
steel safety pin	✓	
plastic bead		✓
cardboard box		✓
copper wire		✓

You would score one mark if you indicated that the steel safety pin is attracted to the magnet, and the copper wire is not. Did you remember that not all metals are magnetic? You would score the second mark if you indicated that the two non-metals, the plastic bead and the cardboard box, were not attracted to the magnet. You were asked to put ticks, did you remember to use them?

CROSS-CHECK   CHAPTER 2